ESSENTIAL
GUIDE TO ANGELS

———————————————— • ————————————————

MARCELLO STANZIONE

Libreria Editrice Vaticana

United States Conference of Catholic Bishops
Washington, DC

First printing, January 2013
ISBN 978-1-60137-197-3

CONTENTS

The Angels According to the Vatican Congregation

own through the centuries, the faithful have translated into various devotional exercises the teaching of the faith in relation to the ministry of angels: the holy angels have been adopted as patrons of cities and corporations; great shrines in their honor have developed such as Mont Saint-Michel in Normandy, San Michele della Chiusa in Piemonte, and San Michele Gargano in Apulia, each appointed with specific feast days; hymns and devotions to the holy angels have also been composed.

Popular piety encompasses many forms of devotion to the guardian angels. St. Basil the Great (†379) taught that "each and every member of the faithful has a guardian angel to protect, guard and guide them through life." This ancient teaching was consolidated by biblical and patristic sources and lies behind many forms of piety. St. Bernard of Clairvaux (†1153) was a great master and a notable promoter of devotion to the guardian angels. For him, they were a proof "that heaven denies us nothing that assists us," and hence, "these celestial spirits have been placed at our sides to protect us, instruct us and to guide us."

Devotion to the holy angels gives rise to a certain form of the Christian life which is characterized by

- Devout gratitude to God for having placed these heavenly spirits of great sanctity and dignity at the service of man
- An attitude of devotion deriving from the knowledge of living constantly in the presence of the holy angels of God
- Serenity and confidence in facing difficult situations, since the Lord guides and protects the faithful in the way of justice through the ministry of his holy angels

Among the prayers to the guardian angels, the Angel of God is especially popular, and is often recited by families at morning and evening prayers, or at the recitation of the *Angelus*.

(*Vatican Congregation for Divine Worship and the Discipline of the Sacraments, Directory on Popular Piety and Liturgy, April 9, 2002, no. 216*)

INTRODUCTION

he term angel is derived from the Hebrew word *mal'ak*, or "messenger," giving origin to the name of a prophet, Malachi, which literally means "Angel of the Lord."

The Greek term closest in meaning to the Hebrew is *angelos*, from which Latin gets *angelus* and hence our word *angel*.

By their nature as purely spiritual beings, angels are the natural intermediaries between God, who by his very essence is Life, and matter, which, in and of itself, has no life.

God, who placed in the angels the image of his infinite perfections, at the same time delegates his sovereignty to them; he has chosen them as interpreters and executors of his wishes in regard to inferior beings.

From a theological point of view, the angels do not have the character of "necessary" beings. God could have created only the material world, ruling and administering it without any intermediary. Instead, he desired to bring these pure intelligences onto the universal plane. Alongside chaotic material he drew up legions of angels to be the living praise of the Creator at the dawn of the world.

The existence of angels is testified to by numerous passages in Holy Scripture. For Catholic doctrine their existence is a dogma of faith, ratified by the Fourth Lateran and First Vatican Councils and reiterated by the *Catechism of the Catholic Church* in article 328.

"With his almighty power from the beginning of time, out of nothing he created both of the orders of creatures: the spiritual one, and the material, that is, the angels and the world, and then man as if a sharer in both the one and the other, composed of both soul and body" (Lat. Coun. IV, 1 *The Catholic Faith*).

I. History of
Devotion to Angels

eneration of angels was accepted very prudently in the Church of the first Christians, since a persistent magical, pagan mentality could risk confusing the angels—intermediary beings between God and the human race—with minor divinities of a new pantheon similar to the pagan one. At the time, gnosticism was positing ever more numerous spiritual beings and seeing emanations of divinity everywhere, resulting in pure polytheism.

In order to avoid deviations and doctrinal misconstruction, the Fathers of the Church tolerated veneration of angels without encouraging it. The first Christians feared Christo-angelology, which was deeply rooted in the sect of the Ebionites who conceived of Christ as a superior angel created by the Father. Even in St. Paul's time there were some heretics in the Christian community of Colossi who considered the angels as the true intermediaries between God and men, thus obscuring Jesus' redeeming work. Once St. Paul became aware of such a heresy, he wrote the Letter to the Colossians, where he decisively affirmed Christ's superiority over the angels. He is the Unbegotten Son of the Father, as opposed to the angels, who were created "through him and for him." This is how those words are to be understood: "Let no one disqualify you, delighting in self-abasement and worship of angels, taking his stand on visions, inflated without reason by his fleshly mind, and not holding closely to the head, from whom the whole body, supported and held together by its ligaments and bonds, achieves the growth that comes from God" (Col 2:18-19).

In the second century AD, **St. Irenaeus** (ca. 130-208) writes in his treatise *Adversus Haereses*, "The Church does nothing either with angelic invocations or with any depraved curiosity, but addresses its prayers in a pure, open manner to the Lord who has made all things." In this text, the saint is combating *theurgia*, that is, the white magic that the gnostics were using together with angelic invocations to work wonders. He therefore affirms that Christians turn only to God from whom all authentic miracles come.

St. Justin (100-162/68), trying to demonstrate to the emperor that Christians are not atheists, states that they pray to the Father, the Son, and the Holy Spirit together with the angelic hosts.

After the Edict of Constantine (313), and with pagan influence on the masses waning, the Church's official position with regard to the veneration of angels grew less rigid.

In the fourth century **St. Eusebius of Caesarea**, in his work *Demonstratio Evangelica*, writes, "Among the heavenly spirits, there are several who, thanks to the saving economy, are sent to mankind; we have learned to know them and venerate them by reason of their dignity and according to their rank, while reserving only for God the homage of our adoration."

Didymus of Alexandria, as early as the fourth century, affirms that there were churches consecrated to God under the name of the archangels. In the city of Constantinople alone there were fifteen churches dedicated to St. Michael.

The Lombards further contributed to an increased devotion to the angels, and in 787 the Second Council of Nicaea recommended to the faithful the veneration of images of the angels.

With **St. Bernard** (1090-1153), the Church witnessed an interesting shift forward. Concerning the heavenly spirits, the saint speaks of "reverence for their person; devotion for their benevolence; trust for their guardianship." Commenting on Psalm 91:11, "For he commands his angels with regard to you, / to guard you wherever you go," he highly praises the veneration of angels, stating, "How much reverence these words should raise up in you, how much devotion you should have, how much trust should inspire you! Reverence for their person; devotion for their benevolence; trust for their guardianship, for they are present, present to you, not only with you but even for you. They are present to protect you, present for your good."

For **St. Bonaventure of Bagnoregio** (1221-1274), the path of maturity in the spiritual life is a journey with a series of encounters with the angels, which leads to union with the Trinitarian God.

From the twelfth century on, and not by chance, the very famous prayer to the guardian angel spread: "Angel of God, my guardian dear, to whom God's love commits me here, ever this day be at my side, to light and guard, to rule and guide. Amen."

In the Middle Ages, the greatest proponents of devotion to angels were the Benedictine monks and, following them, the Franciscans as well. **St. Bernardine of Siena** (1380-1444), in his *Popular Preaching in the Piazza del Campo of Siena*, left us testimony of his continuous and very enthusiastic references to the angels.

The Protestant Reformation and the consequent Catholic Counter-Reformation brought no innovations to the doctrine on angels.

Martin Luther (1483-1546) rejects veneration of angels, as he does that of the saints, in the context of refusing any veneration that is not the adoration rendered to God, and **John Calvin** (1509-1564), in agreement with Luther on the matter, denounces the dry, philosophical speculations that stray from Holy Scripture with their curiosity about the number and nature of angels. Yet Calvin still affirms in the *Institutiones* that "faith in the angels is highly necessary for refuting many errors." Angels constitute "a noble, distinguished part" of creation even if "there is no need to use speculations to go beyond what is appropriate, lest readers stray from the simplicity of the Faith."

A significant sign of the convergence of Protestant and Catholic thought on the matter is the fact that, among the many themes confronted by the **Council of Trent** (1545-1563), there is not even a hint of the question of angels. However, three years after the Council's closing, in 1566, the *Catechism of the Council of Trent for the Use of Parish Priests* was redacted, in which there do appear some references to angels. Although relying completely on a tradition already supported by popular piety, it encourages it, giving it a fresh breath of air. The Tridentine Catechism devotes only one paragraph of few lines to the matter, titled "*De Creatione Angelorum*," which states thus: "From nothing God brought the spiritual world and the innumerable angels to be his dutiful ministers, enriching them with the ineffable gifts of his grace and his great power." It is especially in the fourth part of the Tridentine Catechism, the part dedicated to Sunday prayer, that it speaks more widely about angels and the ways that veneration of them would then develop.

Catholic devotion to the angels reaches its height in the sixteenth and seventeenth centuries. The art historian **Émile Mâle**, in his text on *Religious Art in the Sixteenth Century*, writes, "It is the last celestial hierarchy, that of the angels, that holds the primacy of place in Christian thought and art. In Rome, angels are everywhere: on street corners their grace-filled figures encircle the image of the Madonna before which a lamp burns; on Hadrian's Bridge they bear the instruments of the Passion, their tunics seeming to flutter in the wind like flags in the Tiber breeze; inside the churches they descend from the vaulting to perch on the cornices; in paintings they storm the sky, and there is no Gospel scene in which they do not have a presence. In the seventeenth century those works in which they do not appear seem almost archaic."

In this period, one of the major groups of those promoting devotion to angels were the Jesuits. Well-known is the veneration that both **St. Aloysius of Gonzaga** (1568-1591) and **Blessed Peter Faber** (1506-1546) had for angels; the Jesuit **Pierre Coton** was also a great devotee, as is evident in the prayers of his *Interior Occupation*, and among the many such Jesuits of the era who were apostles of angelic devotion, I would like to remember **Francesco Albertini**, with his *Treatise on the Guardian Angel* (Naples, 1612) as well as **Jacques Hantin** (1665).

From the publication in 1575 of *Treatise and Practical Guide on Devotion to Angels* of **St. Francis Borgia** (1510-1572) until 1650, various Jesuits produced twenty-five works on devotion to angels, not counting the very important work of theologian **Francisco Suárez** (1548-1617), the *De Angelis*, which stands as the most complete synthesis of angelology of the modern age.

The number of treatises rose once again from the end of the seventeenth century through the eighteenth. Only with the Enlightenment and the French Revolution would devotion to angels be hindered by a widespread climate of religious disbelief. Even in the twentieth century, with the spread of liberal theology and exegesis, there has been a marginalization of devotion to angels within the Church, despite the fact that the latest popes have often made references to the heavenly spirits. This has resulted in today's situation, where the majority of publications on angels found in bookstores are sadly of esoteric, occult, New Age, or kabalistic origin.

II. Angels in the Old Testament

ngels are found in the Old Testament every time supernatural manifestations are described. They speak either in their own name or in the Lord's. They show themselves in symbolic forms, such as the mystical animals of Ezekiel, or even in human form. Sometimes this form shines, like in the apparition to Daniel; sometimes it takes on a common human appearance, like the visitors welcomed by Abraham. At other times they are visible only to the eyes of a prophet, while others speak in the very midst of the faithful, as did the Archangel Raphael when he was assisting the young man Tobiah.

In Stephen's discourse before the synagogue, he makes reference to the angel who appeared to Moses in the flames of the burning bush and who spoke to him on the height of Sinai (Acts 7:31, 38). In these two instances the biblical text places the Lord himself at the scene. The conclusion we draw from comparing the two passages is that, when it is said in the Bible that "the Lord appeared" or "the Lord spoke," we should understand "*an angel appeared*," "*an angel spoke in the name of the Lord*." The angels, then, are God's representatives; they are his image, and their action in the Old Testament was universal. St. Paul declares so when he speaks of the Law being "promulgated by angels at the hand of a mediator," who was Moses (Gal 3:19).

Thus, for example, in the account of the Flood we read, "Wisdom again saved it, / piloting the righteous man on frailest wood" (Wis 10:4), meaning the ministry of the angelic spirits who took the helm of the ark on the floodwaters.

Wherever their guidance becomes continuously present, there the People of God are born.

Abraham is in a continual relationship with the angels. They appear near the oak of Mamre under the form of three travelers. One of them represents the Lord, speaking with authority, and the other two seem to be there only to follow his orders. They are headed toward Sodom and bring Lot out of the midst of this infamous city doomed to divine vengeance (Gn 18 and 19).

This angelic protection extends also to his servant girl Hagar: the first time, when a heavenly messenger comes to announce Ishmael's destiny, and the second, when he shows her the well in the desert when her child is about to die of thirst (Gn 16:7; 21:17).

Angels watch over the servant girl's son just as they do the free woman's son. One of them stops the hand of Abraham just as it is raised to sacrifice Isaac (Gn 22:11). An angel also acts as an invisible intermediary at this patriarch's wedding to Rebecca (Gn 24).

Jacob is no less familiar with these mysterious apparitions. Asleep on a rock at Bethel, in a dream he sees a symbolic ladder rising high above his head; angels are climbing up and down on it. When he is near Laban, an angel warns him that the time has come for him to return to Canaan.

On the road, he sees legions of angels and cries out, "This is God's encampment" (Gn 32:3). Then he wrestles all night with a being in human form, which, according to Hosea, we are to recognize as an angel (Hos 12:34). On his deathbed, already blind but enlightened from on high, he invokes upon the heads of his grandsons, Joseph's sons Ephraim and Manasseh, the angel who rescued him safe and sound from all dangers (Gn 28:12; 31:11; 32:1; 48:16).

The angels who watched over the patriarchs and guided them in all their ways watch also over God's People, grown to maturity and leaving Egypt.

An angel—no doubt the angel of Jacob—walks with the cloud at the front line of the Hebrew emigrants. Then, to defend them from Pharaoh's pursuing hoards, he passes to the rear guard (Ex 14:19). At various points, an angel is announced to Moses as the people's guide toward the Promised Land. Not only, then, is there the visible guide—Moses—but an invisible one always at his side—the angel of the Lord. Nor does anyone doubt that it was precisely this angel who conversed with this great prophet in God's name.

This general behavior does not hinder special interventions on the part of the heavenly spirits. Perhaps nothing is as strange as the biblical account of the angel, with his sword raised aloft, who causes Balaam's donkey to open her mouth and warn the false prophet in a human voice about the danger he is risking (Nm 22-36). The angel responsible for God's People does not end his duty once the Hebrews are settled in the Promised Land. Instead, he makes himself visible to the eyes of the people and reprimands them for lack of obedience to the Lord's orders. The people break down in sobs at this new way of being dealt with, and the place where this scene takes place becomes known as "the place of weepers" (see Jgs 2:5).

The angelic interventions continue throughout the time of the Judges. One angel appears to Gideon announcing that he will exterminate Madian and, as a sign that he speaks the truth, sets fire to the Israelite's sacrifice (Jgs 6:11-22). Soon afterward, an angel announces the birth of Samson to Manoah's wife and then to Manoah himself, before ascending back to God in the flames of the altar (Jgs 13:3-21).

Holy Scripture does not expressly mention visible action on the part of angels in the dramatic story of David, but how could it be denied that the king speaks from experience when he sings, "For he commands his angels with regard to you, / to guard you wherever you go. / With their hands they shall support you, / lest you strike your foot against a stone. / You can tread upon the asp and the viper, / trample the lion and the dragon" (Ps 91:11-13).

The angels are also the ministers of God's scourges. While David's reign was coming to an end, he committed a sin of vanity that displeased God. He was punished: God sent an angel who smote 70,000 Israelites with the plague, but God stopped when moved to pity by David's repentance. The angel put back his sword (2 Sm 24:25).

The prophet Elijah was placed in the angels' custody: it is an angel who has him eat the miraculous bread that sustains him on his forty-day journey; and it is an angel again who orders him to give Ahaziah and Ahaz the news of their imminent deaths (1 Kgs 19:5; 2 Kgs 1:16).

Elisha's eye follows the movements of the heavenly hosts that come to help the city, where the cavalry and chariots of the king of Syria surround them; the Lord grants his prayer that his servant should also be able to see such a marvelous spectacle: a heavenly cavalry with chariots of fire (2 Kgs 6:17).

The angel of death comes to Hezekiah's aid while he is being besieged by Sennacherib; in one night the angel strews the ground with 185,000 enemy bodies.

During the Captivity, the angels follow the Israelites into exile. Here the well-known story of Tobiah takes place: the Archangel Raphael, in human form, enters the scene to perform a whole series of touching miracles on behalf of this family that has been blessed by God; this is the unseen action of the heavenly spirits made visible, palpable. The whole book of Tobit is a poem to the guardian angels.

Judith, who fights for the freedom of her fatherland, testifies that an angel led her and brought her back, not only safe and sound, but clean from defilement (Jdt 13:20).

The angels intervene constantly in the stories and prophecies of Daniel. They come down to help the young men in the furnace and guard them from the devouring flames; they descend with the prophet into the lion's den and shut the mouths of those untamed beasts; they transport the prophet Habakkuk to him, who gives Daniel something to eat (Dn 3:49; 6:22; 14:32). It is Daniel, the man of desires, of humble, pure heart, who has the vision of an angel in all his glory—he is left shaken and faints. The angel reassures him and leads him into the council of the heavenly spirits and of God himself (Dn 10).

The assistance of the angels is notable even in Maccabees. Judas Maccabeus beseeches the Lord to deign to send an angel to save Israel—a touching prayer that God hears and answers visibly! In fact, he sees walking before him a horseman dressed in white and brandishing golden weapons. Before this, in the most heated moment of the battle, the enemy had seen five gleaming horsemen descending from heaven, then surrounding and covering the valiant warrior: two of them protected him on the right and left, warding off the enemy arrows and hurling lightning bolts that sowed terror and death everywhere (2 Mc 10:29-30; 11:6).

III. Angels in the New Testament

ome Fathers of the Church tell us that the angelic apparitions of the Old Testament are preludes to the Incarnation of the Son of God. These visions of celestial messengers in human form both announce and prefigure the great and definitive manifestation of the Son of God made man, yet they do not end with his arrival on earth. Jesus came to restore the order of grace, yet without destroying the natural order. His great, redeeming mediation has not nullified the natural mediation of the heavenly spirits. They always remain the intermediaries between God and man. Their mission is woven harmoniously into the work of redemption, as is easily seen from a large number of Gospel and apostolic events.

An angel had announced the birth of Samson. The Archangel Gabriel in like manner announces the birth of St. John the Baptist. Then he goes to find the Virgin of Nazareth, as an ambassador of the Most Holy Trinity, and asks her consent to become the Mother of the Son of God. The angel thus becomes the *paranymph* of the marriage between the Word and humanity (Lk 1). An angel, perhaps Gabriel again, announces to Joseph the mystery that has taken place in the womb of his chaste spouse and dispels the heart-wrenching apprehension that tortures his heart (Mt 1:20).

On the day of the Son of God's birth, it is an angel who announces the Good News to the shepherds. Heaven seems to meld with earth around the cave of the newborn, so numerous are the angelic hosts that rejoice and sing of the great marvel of the Child God (Lk 2:9-15). The Holy Family is surrounded by angels who serve and protect them.

At the side of the visible leader—once Moses, now Joseph—stands the invisible leader, the angel of the Lord, and the invisible one guides the visible. An angel then appeared to Joseph and warned him, as once with Jacob, to return to the land of Israel (Mt 2:13, 29).

The Lord, having become an adult, does not refuse to be ministered to by angels. With his incarnation he had descended below angelic nature (Ps 8; Heb 2:7, 9). By becoming man, he had placed himself in a position not only to accept the angels' service but even to need it. In fact, he made recourse to them in two specific instances.

The first was at the time of his fasting and temptation in the desert. At first, Jesus is struggling with the Devil, but he soon triumphs over him and forces him to withdraw. "Then," the Gospel tells us, "behold, angels came and ministered to him" (Mt 4:11; Mk

1:13). What does this angelic service consist in? They comforted the Savior's pure humanity severely weakened by his fasting, tested by the insults of the evil spirit.

The second instance was the Savior's painful agony. Jesus was in the throes of sadness, fear, and overwhelming revulsion. He was undergoing a depression of such force as to consider death; it was crushed by such unspeakable anguish that he sweated blood. But suddenly an angel appears to him from heaven, "to strengthen him" (Lk 22:43). This is an important intervention. Angelic nature comes to the aid of human nature, beaten down and agonizing; an angel strengthens Jesus, who suffers as man; he is cut off from all sense of union with his Father; his humanity, stretched to the limits, was sustained thanks to the aid of the angelic spirits.

Given that they watched over the Head, it is not surprising that they should be called to watch over the Body. They protect the fledgling Church, and announce the Lord's glorious Resurrection to the pious women and Apostles.

At the Ascension, the angels are again there, under human form. They reassure, encourage, and console the Apostles (Acts 1:10). As they did around the tomb, they wear white garments, symbols of joy.

When the Church comes out from the Cenacle, the angels work, so to speak, with the Apostles; when they are imprisoned, they break their chains (Acts 5:19). They arrange providential encounters with the pagans for them. One of these heavenly spirits tells Philip the deacon to head towards the street of Gaza where he will find the eunuch of the queen of Ethiopia (Acts 8:27). Another will order the centurion Cornelius to go find St. Peter (Acts 10:3).

When the Church is threatened with being beheaded in the person of Peter, having fallen into the hands of Herod, it is an angel who miraculously frees him and brings him back to the Church that has been in prayer and in tears (Acts 12:7). Divine vengeance is brought down on the persecutor through the angel, his minister: he dies in horrific convulsions, eaten alive by worms (Acts 12:23).

Even St. Paul is protected by angels. They follow him in all of his apostolic journeys. In the storm related in Acts, an angel appears to the apostle and assures him that no harm will befall either him or his fellow passengers (Acts 27:23).

Such is the angels' role in the Church's foundation and first developments. They surround it with close protection. They set up the encounters that the Apostles will have with these "children of God," as St. John calls them (1 Jn 3:1), who were spread throughout the world, and whom the Apostles were trying to gather into one Church.

IV. Christ and His Angels

I n Christ, the two parts of the supernatural world are united: the angelic and the human. He is King of the angels as well as of men, responsible for bringing all of creation back to the Father. St. Paul, in fact, writes that Christ is "as far superior to the angels / as the name he has inherited is more excellent than theirs. For to which of the angels did God ever say: 'You are my son; this day I have begotten you'?" (Heb 1:4-5; Ps 2:7). And again: "I will be a father to him, and he shall be a son to me" (Heb 1:6; 2 Sm 7:14). "And again, when he leads the first-born into the world, he says: 'Let all the angels of God worship him'" (Heb 1:6; Ps 97:7). " . . . To sum up all things in Christ, in heaven and on earth" (Eph 1:10).

Busying themselves around Christ, then, are *his* angels, *ministers*, servants, twelve legions of whom could intervene at the merest signal (Dn 7:10; Mt 4:11; 26:53).

The angels are always present in Christ's life.

Gabriel announces John the Baptist's birth to Zechariah (Lk 1:11). Then there is the Annunciation to Mary, God's request for consent from the future

Mother of the Savior: the pivotal scene in the drama of Creation (Lk 1:26-38).

Again the angels are there to calm Joseph's anxiety and to warn him to flee to Egypt (Mt 1:20; 2:13). To the shepherds they describe the Child-God lying in a manger, and reveal to all the key to the mystery of the Incarnation: the glory of God and peace given to mankind (Lk 2:9-15). From the very beginning of Jesus' public life, they reappear in the Gospel, calling to mind the vision of Jacob (Jn 1:51); angels serve Christ after the temptation (Mt 4:11). In Gethsemane as well, in his most tragic hour, when Jesus' sorrow becomes so intense that he sweats blood, an angel comes to comfort him (Lk 22:43).

Easter: the Resurrection. While true that one of the angels terrifies the guards as he rolls the stone away from the tomb, the others, dressed in joyous white, announce the good news to Mary of Magdala and the pious women (Mt 28:1-7; Jn 20:11-13). At another time they will bring closure to Christ's earthly mission after the Ascension and inaugurate the Church's time of expectation: "They said, 'Men of Galilee, why are you standing there looking at the sky? This Jesus who has been taken up from you into heaven will return in the same way as you have seen him going into heaven'" (Acts 1:11).

Angels are Christ's servants as well as his collaborators in the work of redemption. It is they who free

Peter (Acts 10:36) and instruct Cornelius (Acts 12:7-11). In fact: "Are they not all ministering spirits sent to serve, for the sake of those who are to inherit salvation?" (Heb 1:14).

These are loving, concerned servants who rejoice with the Good Shepherd over the flock that has been lost and then found (Lk 15:1-10). Revelation could not help but finish with a look at the final consummation where there will only exist two separate camps: angels and the elect on one side, demons and the damned on the other. Christ had already made them witnesses to and executors of his judgments, responsible for separating the good wheat from the weeds, the good fish from the bad (Mt 13:24-30, 36-43, 47-56). In symbolic language, Revelation describes them as united to mankind in their common, eternal praise of Christ and the Lamb: "I looked again and heard the voices of many angels who surrounded the throne and the living creatures and the elders. They were countless in number, and they cried out in a loud voice: 'Worthy is the Lamb that was slain / to receive power and riches, wisdom and strength, / honor and glory and blessing'" (Rev 5:11-12).

V. Angels and the Church

Angels surround the Church defending her, preparing her for the great day of her eternal wedding when they shall form her procession as Bride of the Lamb.

The mission of the angels is one of the natural order. Even before Baptism, a child coming into the world is provided with a guardian angel. "Great must be the dignity of souls," says St. Jerome, "for each of them to have, from birth, an angel dedicated to guarding them." If the angels' duty to human souls is of the natural order in and of itself, they perform it with a supernatural end. For this reason, St. Paul calls them "ministering spirits sent to serve, for the sake of those who are to inherit salvation" (Heb 1:14). This Pauline phrase places the angels' mission in its true light.

The angels are placed in charge of protecting human creatures—ignorant, weak, or needy. Yet, while caring diligently for their protégés even on a purely natural plane, they work tirelessly to direct and guide our earthly, existential journey toward the "inheritance of salvation." And so, when chosen to the guardianship of a non-Catholic, the angel will try to open his or her heart and make easier the ways that will bring the soul to the Christian faith and to Baptism.

In union with the apostolic men, the angels work for the edification of the Church. After preparing the Apostles' encounters with unbelievers and sinners, they lend support to their words with secret inspirations. We have seen them at work in the Acts of the Apostles, these celestial agents, these unseen intermediaries. What they accomplished then, they continue to do without ceasing. Are there not a thousand coincidences in the work of saving souls that would remain inexplicable were we not to see the action of these ministering spirits we call angels behind it all? The primary duty of the angelic spirits, then, is to strive to gather these *living stones* with which the Church is built. A second duty is to make the prayers of the Church rise to God. A third is to watch over her and to protect her from her enemies.

Revelation, which is the prophetic story of the Church, paints us a very expressive picture of the varying ministries of the good angels.

"And I saw that the seven angels who stood before God were given seven trumpets," says St. John. "Another angel came and stood at the altar, holding a gold censer. He was given a great quantity of incense to offer, along with the prayers of all the holy ones, on the gold altar that was before the throne. The smoke of the incense along with the prayers of the holy ones went up before God from the hand of the angel. Then the angel took the censer, filled it with burning coals from the altar, and hurled it down to the earth. There were peals of thunder, rumblings, flashes of lightning, and an earthquake. The seven angels who were holding the seven trumpets prepared to blow them" (Rev 8:2-6).

Every sounding of the angelic trumpets causes the earth to shake. Later, several different angels appear: one who preaches to the people in a voice resembling the roar of a lion, one holding a sharpened scythe, one with power over fire. Finally seven heavenly spirits come upon the scene, one by one emptying out the seven cups of God's wrath (Rev 16).

The holy angel's duty, that of assisting and defending the Church during its earthly pilgrimage, is rather clearly and vividly described in these pages, pages whose frightening aspect we should not foolishly downplay, but where we can also draw from its comforting side.

Assigning the seven trumpets to the seven angels indicates that these are in charge of sealing, opening, and developing, so to speak, the great ages of humanity.

Yet we suddenly see an angel called to perform a priestly ministry, analogous to that carried out by the Levite in the Old Law: he takes up the incense representing the prayers of the saints, burns it, and releases its perfume before God's throne.

This passage reveals to us a very important truth: the angels have the mission of presenting our prayers to God. "The Son of Man saves," says St. Hilary, "the angels see God, and the angels of children preside at the prayers of the faithful. That there is an angelic presence is not up for discussion. Every day the angels offer to God, through Christ, the prayers of the faithful. Great danger lies in mistreating one of these little ones, whose desires and pleas are presented to the eternal, unseen God by the swift and magnificent ministry of the angels."

VI. ANGELS AND THE END OF THE WORLD

On earth, angels perform the ministry of justice. Among the officials of the heavenly court is the Angel of Death. Though Scripture does not indicate it clearly, this angel passed through the land of Egypt on the night of Passover, bringing death to the firstborn of the Egyptians. It was he who executed the sentence punishing the Israelites for a sin of vanity committed by King David and who covered Jerusalem's surrounding land with the corpses of Sennacherib's army. He struck King Herod just when he reveled in arrogance, thinking himself a god.

St. Gregory the Great caught sight of an angel above Hadrian's Tomb—now Castel Sant'Angelo—slipping his sword back in its sheath, indicating that the plague had ended. Revelation confirms this role of the heavenly spirits as ministers of divine justice. Seven celestial spirits, God's great avengers, empty out the seven cups upon the earth.

In Matthew's Gospel, Jesus sets forth and explains several parables. In one of these, the world is likened to a field where weeds and wheat are growing together. Who will harvest that field? Jesus says, "The harvesters are the angels." And just as the harvesters will separate the weeds and throw them on the fire, while the wheat is placed in the granaries, so will the angels sent by the Son of Man remove the makers of scandal and iniquity from the Kingdom of God, and "they will throw them into the fiery furnace, where there will be wailing and grinding of teeth. Then the righteous will shine like the sun in the kingdom of their Father" (Mt 13:42-43).

Jesus uses parables to highlight the truth, yet he also expresses himself directly: "And he will send out his angels with a trumpet blast, and they will gather his elect from the four winds, from one end of the heavens to the other" (Mt 24:31).

According to the Gospels the angels will have the great ministry of bringing resolution to the drama of the end times. Such a ministry can be divided into three stages: before judgment, during judgment, and after judgment.

First, the Gospel text tells us, "the angels will go out." This *exit* of the angels will likewise be their manifestation in visible form—thunderous and formidable. They will sound the trumpet and cry out in a loud voice. The angels will make themselves felt as much as seen: their voice will have the power to wake the dead in their tombs; they shall assemble the chosen ones like a commander gathers his scattered troops at the sound of the trumpet; they will herd the impenitent reprobates into one place and be placed in charge of preparations for judgment.

They will *then* be made the counselors of the Eternal Judge and will assist at the trial. "I tell you, everyone who acknowledges me before others," says Jesus, "the Son of Man will acknowledge before the angels of God" (Lk 12:8).

Finally they intervene as executors of judgment. Jesus makes it clearly understood with the parable of the harvest. The harvesters separate the weeds from the good grain, and while they cast the weeds into the fire, they carry the grain to the granaries. This is what the angels will also do with the elect and the reprobates, and they will act with marvelous, infallible discernment. The order will be carried out at the angels' hands, even in that horrifying place described as "the dark, disordered land where darkness is the only light" (Jb 10:22). Those who have committed similar sins will be *bound* together in the fright and desperation of one same punishment.

The angels will joyfully accompany the elect into paradise.

In the *Last Judgment* painted by Blessed Fra Angelico the area occupied by the damned is chaotic, and their expressions are full of horror and hopelessness, while in the wing taken up by the elect there is beauty and harmony. Angels embrace or kiss the souls at the threshold of paradise.

The angel introduces the elect into heaven, and both of them enter into God as into the infinite ocean of their shared beatitude.

VII. THE NATURE OF ANGELS

There exist three species of spirits: the **human**, the **angelic**, and the **Divine**, which is the Creator of all things. These spirits move in three spheres that can be defined as concentric. The first sphere, that of the shortest radius, is the sphere of human intelligence. The second, which widens outside of the first, higher and longer beyond comparison, is that which inhabits and fills angelic nature. Finally the third, which contains the other two in infinite dimensions, is the sphere of inaccessible Light, which is the place proper to God the Creator, that of the Most Blessed and Adorable Trinity.

Now, man's knowledge in and of itself is limited to the sphere that it inhabits. It has human things as its specific field. For as much as it elevates its reasoning, it will still not have a clear, distinct vision of the spiritual world. When it seeks to form an idea of it for itself, the images of sensible things come in the way of the soul's eye and these purely spiritual objects; so it can only distinguish them very confusedly, as one makes out distant objects at a great distance through a cloudy lens. In a word, in order to know God perfectly, it would be necessary to be God himself; to know the angels, it would be necessary to be an angel. Man, who tries to penetrate the secrets of angelic nature, will always come short of the truth. He will be like the astronomer exploring the spaces of light where the stars move. Can he boast of having an absolutely exact knowledge? Not in the least. Nevertheless, his observations are neither sterile nor useless.

Thus man discovers in the angel the reflection of an ideal beauty that descends directly from God, from him whom St. Gregory of Nazianzus calls the "first Light," the "first Splendor." "The angels," he says, "are like a brook, a small stream of the first Light; they are the second splendors at the service of the first Splendor."

An angel is a pure spirit. He is not composed, like us, of two associated substances; God has not made of him, according to the expression of St. Gregory the Great, an inexplicable mixture of spirit and mud: "*investigabili dispositione miscuit spiritum et litum.*" He is a pure spiritual substance, which admits no mixture of the corporeal element, even the most indistinct.

An angel has nothing corporeal about him; he is pure spirit but is also a created spirit. In other words, he is infinitely distant from that pure Spirit who is the Creating Spirit.

Creating Spirit, created spirit: in these two terms there is a difference that cannot be explained except by difference that exists between a living being and an inanimate image. If an angel is close to God by his quality as a pure spirit, by his quality as a created spirit he is close to man and remains close to man, since the distance that separates him from God is immeasurable.

Insofar as it is created spirit, we consider angelic nature essentially constrained and limited: limited in its essence, limited in its power, limited in its field of operations.

VIII. Angelic Faculties

Intelligence and will are faculties of the soul, similar to two wings that transport it to higher planes. The angelic spirit is obviously provided with these wings. In the angel, they are all the more quick and powerful due to his being pure spirit. Between human intelligence and will, and angelic intelligence and will, the difference is the same as that between the folded wings of an insect and the widely outstretched wings of eagles.

The numerous imperfections of man do not exist in **angelic intelligence**.

As a pure spirit, an angel has an intelligence that never sleeps: from the first moment of his existence, it produces an action that it has not formed, yet is. One instant is enough for an angel to gain knowledge, just as it only takes one glance for a human placed on a height to take in an immense horizon.

This does not mean that an angel's knowledge cannot be increased, yet it expands without suffering, with no effort, to the objects presented to it and that enter into his field of vision, so to speak. St. Thomas does not shy from affirming that, taken in and of itself and relatively to its natural object, this knowledge is immune from all error, because in a single stroke it reaches into the depth of the object and embraces it in all of its qualities.

It does not proceed through a laborious reasoning process but springs from a sure intuition. An angel knows everything spiritually, even material things—the opposite of man, who knows everything materially, even spiritual things: the difference is great.

St. Thomas, in fact, imagines that between an angel's knowledge and that of the most knowledgeable human being there is a difference even greater than that between the knowledge of the most intelligent man and that of the most ignorant man.

Angelic will follows its intelligence and draws the spirit toward the object whose beauty is revealed to it. Human intelligence being as uncertain as it is, human will then also turns out hesitant; we see it attach itself to an object, then leave it; it is free, but its freedom is diminished by the impulse of the passions born of sensual appetite. If, as we have seen, angelic intelligence differs from human intelligence by its readiness and the surety of its conceptions, angelic will differs from ours by the energy and inexplicable tenacity of its resolutions. The angel is unquestionably free, and his freedom is more detached than ours; being accessible only to the attraction of immaterial goods, it is not susceptible to these fluctuations that result from those opposing tendencies born in the spirit and in the flesh.

Being free with a superior freedom, the angel makes his own self-determination for one purpose or another. He makes this determination with such an absolute strength of will that the decision becomes immediately irrevocable. Moreover, an angel is not impeccable. Being absolutely free from falling is a privilege only of divine nature. Every created being can fall away from his Creator, just as, with grace, it can perfect itself by drawing close to him.

IX. The Creation of Angels

According to the Fourth Lateran Council, the creation of the angels coincided with that of the creation of chaotic material and the world's first elements: an instantaneous apparition of myriads of angelic spirits forming an immense choir of praise for the Eternal God.

This multitude of spirits was not a flurry of immaterial beings spread out haphazardly in infinite space. From the beginning, the angelic world entered the world organized, brought out of nothing as a well-arrayed army. These pure intelligences were distributed into three different hierarchies, which were in turn divided into three choirs. The superior hierarchy communicated the overabundance of divine goodness to the middle one, the middle to the lower, while the nine choirs, like new worlds of light enveloped in an immense sphere, gravitated around the perfect center where God was.

The hierarchies were perfect by nature, possessing the innate joy inspired by their powerful faculties. They knew each other as they compenetrated each other. They knew God, not in the impenetrable mystery of his essence, but in his glorious qualities as the immortal, Creating Spirit. Their gaze tore the veil off of material creation and, within the divine radius that sustains it and makes it fertile, grasped the laws that, in full wisdom, gave it order. Nothing escaped the eye of these spirits, and one instant was enough for them to take possession of the intellectual world that was their element.

At the same time, their will underwent an equally magnificent impulse. It exulted in God in unison with the very movement that brought it to joy. It adored him in himself and in his works. This first impulse was a consequence of the creative act; it was good but not meritorious, since it resulted from God the Creator's impulse and not from the creature's free determination.

It would have been of little value for the angel to be created with the perfection of his natural faculties if he were not also elevated to the state of grace. The Creator deigned to give this capsule of supreme perfection to the first and most beautiful work of his hands. "Simultaneously," says St. Augustine, "the angelic nature was created and grace was spread among the angelic spirits." They were made for supernatural beatitude: even from the first moment of their existence, they were placed on a path to reach this beatitude, consisting in the intuitive vision of God.

No more so than with man, the angel could not pass through the veil where God conceals himself if not by the supernatural movement of grace. Just like us, he needed the freely given virtues of faith, hope, and charity, without which no creature can aspire to the glory of heaven.

God, then, as he created them, gave the angelic spirits grace; he gave them the supernatural graces that are the necessary consequence of it. Within them he placed this seed of glory and beatitude.

What this infusion of grace in these pure spirits was is impossible even to conceive. Finding no obstacle in them, freely penetrating these transparent natures, it spread from the center of their being into their noble faculties like a stream of splendors. Referring to this infusion of supernatural life, St. Augustine said of the angels: "No sooner were they made, than they were made light." Because the first light was aimed into these spirits like a sunray into a diamond, it produced a wide array of fiery lights.

They did not enjoy the vision of God but were plunged into the luminous cloud where he conceals himself. They knew him by faith, in the mystery of the Trinity of Persons, with a clairvoyance that we do not have. They did not possess God, and God still sat among them as on a throne from on high, from which he presided over all of creation.

They were not yet in the definitive heaven, the place proper to the divine vision and the home of the blessed, but rather in a spiritual paradise that acted as its entryway. It is in the delights of this paradise that the prophet depicts Lucifer before his sin. "You were a seal of perfection, / full of wisdom, perfect in beauty. / In Eden, the garden of God, you lived; / precious stones of every kind were your covering: / Carnelian, topaz, and beryl, / chrysolite, onyx, and jasper, / sapphire, garnet, and emerald. / Their mounts and settings / were wrought in gold, / fashioned for you the day you were created. / With a cherub I placed you; / I put you on the holy mountain of God, / where you walked among fiery stones. / Blameless were you in your ways / from the day you were created, / until evil was found in you" (Ez 28:12-15).

X. ANGELS IN HUMAN FORM

he Old Testament is filled with angelic apparitions. Some take on a transitory character, like that of Gideon's angel, while others remain over time. In this last case, the heavenly spirits speak with mankind and make themselves publically visible. Such a case is that of the three angels who came to meet Abraham; as is that of St. Raphael when he descended to help the family of Tobit. These latter apparitions are of particular interest to us, because it is clear that angels, manifesting themselves this way, had taken on a visible body, material and palpable like our own. We have to then ask ourselves: to what degree do the angels bond themselves with a material body?

At first, these rather apparently human apparitions, found in Holy Scripture, are irrefutable proof that material obeys the will of angels, that they can compress and mold it more deftly than an artist molds clay, infuse it with a living semblance, and, finally, adopting it like a garment, use it as an instrument.

Angels do not bond themselves with material bodies in order to complete such a mission in the same way that our soul is bonded to a body, creating one sole being. Between our soul and body there is a substantial link that fuses these two substances in the bond of one same nature; between angels and these bodies of theirs, which they take on temporarily, the bond is only accidental. Our clothing does not form a union with us; the tool we use does not pertain to our nature as man. The bodies taken on by angels are like garments under which they make themselves visible, simple instruments used with great dexterity.

Since the union of the angelic spirits with these loan-bodies, so to speak, is not a *vital* union, it performs no *organic* function. They seem to eat, they even really do eat, but—forgive us for this necessary detail—they do not digest food. "Even though you saw me eat and drink," says the Archangel Raphael, "I did not eat or drink anything; what you were seeing was a vision" (Tb 12:19).

Once finished with their temporary mission, the angels dissolve the bodies they had assumed into impalpable elements. They would disappear like a lightening bolt, as did the Archangel Raphael (Tb 12:21).

Since they are not substantially bonded with these material bodies, angels can act spiritually and from a distance on other bodies and beings. Thus, while Raphael accompanies Tobiah in Babylon, at the same time he captures Asmodeus and goes off to tie him up in the desert of Egypt. This archangel's sphere of activity could extend to another place altogether.

This long-distance action should be enough to convince us that the angels live completely independent of the bodies they appear in to the righteous of the Ancient Covenant and that there is no substantial union.

With the New Covenant, it seems that these apparitions have ceased. Since their principle goal was to announce and symbolize, under perceivable form, Jesus' Incarnation, it is no wonder that they are neither as frequent nor as public as before. On the other hand, we cannot say that they will not happen again. Everything leads us to believe that near the end times the supernatural phenomena of angelic apparitions—both good and evil—will happen again on a wide scale.

For an angel, union with a material body is an accidental, transitory state that does not change his general relations with the visible world, that does not alter his properties as a uniquely spiritual being. As such, he has the power to act on bodies in a determined sphere, to put matter's most latent energies into motion. This action is as impenetrable as it is interior, and is just as much in harmony with the nature of things. Seeing the Archangel Raphael move and act as a human, Tobit's family said, "He is a man; he is Azariah, son of the great Hananiah!" Contemplating the order of nature, so beautiful and constant, so varied and yet so uniform, we say: "It is nature!" We do not discern the angel's action; it adapts so well to the natural properties of beings without ever harming them that, in imitation of Divine action, it fills everything and yet nowhere reveals itself.

XI. The Great Battle in Heaven

hen war broke out in heaven; Michael and his angels battled against the dragon. The dragon and its angels fought back, but they did not prevail and there was no longer any place for them in heaven. The huge dragon, the ancient serpent, who is called the Devil and Satan, who deceived the whole world, was thrown down to earth, and its angels were thrown down with it" (Rev 12:7-9).

Not long after their creation, there was a huge rift between the angels: those who revolted against God and the others who bowed down to him with love. These opposing attitudes, these movements into opposite camps took the form of a true battle, each side trying to make their opinion prevail and gathering the greatest number of followers. The good ones on God's side gained the victory, whether due to their numbers or to the power of their efforts, and the opposing side found itself shut out of heaven.

How could such an evil tendency come about in the midst of the angels, pure, sublime creatures that they are?

All angels were created perfect according to their nature and adorned with the grace that brought them to God. St. Augustine says, "God had given them an upright will, so that they would adhere to him with a chaste love." They did not have to have the free determination of their will to follow the movement of grace that incited them. They then entered into possession of God, seen and contemplated face to face.

In the initial moment of their existence, they all exulted in God their Creator. "Where were you when I founded the earth? . . .While the morning stars sang together / and all the sons of God shouted for joy?" (Jb 38:4, 7). These morning stars, these sons of God were the angels in the brightness of their resplendent nature that sprang from God.

This exultation brought no merit. It preceded any free determination. It was the consequence and reaction of the creating impulse.

It was no longer than an instant, but an instant of different duration than the fleeting moments that measure our earthly existence. All of God's eternity has but one single moment that never ends. Every moment of the angels' life is of a duration that could be equivalent to centuries. This moment must have been quite long, since it is said of the rebellious angel: "You walked among fiery stones . . . until evil was found in you."

This moment passed: the angels regained their composure and self-control. They were able to act as free creatures and decide on the aim of their existence.

They were not enticed, as we are, by the attraction of inferior goods, but were faced with a dual choice: on one side, God, whose beauty attracted them powerfully; on the other, their own nature, whose beauty also had its seduction. Pride themselves in God, or in themselves; seek their supreme happiness in God, or want to find it in themselves. Such were the two ends for which the angels' free will had to make its explicit choice.

Could their choice be doubtful? Did these pure spirits not understand that the truth for them was to offer themselves to the Uncreated Beauty? To recognize that they were nothing in comparison to him who is all and, detaching themselves from the deceiving attractions of creatures, to fling themselves into God with one powerful movement? In a word, to put their aim and supreme happiness into him and him alone? Without a doubt, with their shining intelligence, they understood that their indefeasible duty was to prefer God to themselves, yet several, drunk with vain pride, did not step into line.

At that very moment, there was a rupture in heaven. In the solemn silence that followed that first angelic jubilation, from the height of one of the upper hierarchies a cry for revolt was heard. It was Lucifer who shouted: "Above the stars of God / I will set up my throne . . . I will ascend above the tops of the clouds; / I will be like the Most High!" (Is 14:13, 14).

The cry met a formidable response. One part of the angels repeated the anthem. Evil had entered the cosmos by the depraved will of a creature.

At that same instant another shout was lifted by the glorious St. Michael: "Who is like God? Who is similar to God?" A shout of triumphant obedience, of victorious protest, of complete love for God. It overpowered the uproar caused by Lucifer and the rebels, rallying the faithful cohorts of the angels who shouted it in a clamorous din.

Lucifer was thwarted in his plan to win over all of the angels in his rebellion in order to make himself the god of the angelic realm. He was foiled by St. Michael's protest, was unable to withstand the light that radiated from the faithful Legions, and plunged down backwards, vanquished by the light. "There was no longer any place for them in heaven" (Rev 12:8).

And thus, for the angelic realm, a distinction began between the two opposing cities: Babylon and Jerusalem. "Two loves," said St. Augustine, "made two cities: one, Jerusalem, love for God unto denial of self; the other, Babylon, love for self unto denial of God." The faithful angels had loved God to the point of self-denial; the rebel angels had loved themselves to the point of despising God.

XII. Spiritual Light and Spiritual Darkness

S t. Augustine describes the consequences of the choice made by the angels: "The first, kneeling before the Word, became light; the second, dwelling on their own selves, became night." Light and darkness cannot subsist together: it was an irrevocable division. Spiritual light—that is, the good angels—ascended to that spring of pure light that is God; spiritual darkness—the evil angels—were thrust into the netherworld.

Those good ones were immediately inducted into the highest heaven where God can be seen; the evil ones were instead sent swiftly headlong into the abyss of hell.

With their act of submission, the first group merited possessing God in face-to-face contemplation, while the second merited that eternal exclusion from God that we call damnation.

One single good act placed the first group into the joy of supreme beatitude; one single evil act plunged the second into damnation with its whole cortege of endless evils. It was as quick as lightening, as the Lord said: "I have observed Satan fall like lightning from the sky" (Lk 10:18).

We can be dumbfounded by this frightful punishment, as swift as the prideful thought that provoked it and left no room for repentance. It proves that God owes the sinner nothing but justice, that he is not obliged to give anyone time for penance or pardon. If he deigns to grant it to us poor, human creatures, it is only out of pure, free goodness.

The instantaneousness and irrevocability of this punishment can also be explained by what has been stated about angelic nature. The intelligence of angels does not suffer the fumbling of human reason: it hits directly at an object's core. Their will does not undergo our characteristic hesitation, but it attaches itself wholly to its goal with indomitable energy and irreversible tenacity. Thanks to this intellectual incisiveness, to this power of will, the angels could decide their whole life in one single act, establishing—with no looking back—their eternal destiny, whether blessed or damned.

In their cry of submission to God, the angels placed all their intelligence, all their free will, all their incomparable energy, all their being, firmly and irrevocably into goodness and into God—just as the evil angels, in their cry of revolt, had thrown aside all of their beautiful nature with their innate vigor. From that moment on, the latter would be forever marked by the evil they had freely chosen. In either one, the act was *definitive*.

And so there were three moments in the history of the angels. The first was that of their creation and of their praise-filled jubilation; the second when, gaining self-control, they freely made their definitive choice; and finally, the third moment, which marked their eternal recompense or eternal retribution. The second was absolutely instantaneous.

Aristotle expresses a thought that St. Thomas adopts in his *Summa Theologiae*: "There are some beings that reach their end through various, successive movements." These are human creatures, who generally arrive at the supreme joy of heaven by accumulating works of virtue. "There are others," continues the Greek philosopher, "who reach their end with very simple movements very small in number." These are the angels, who merited their final beatitude with a single act of virtue that contained the quintessence of all other possible acts. "Finally," he concludes, "there is one Being that possesses its end without any movement." This Being is clearly God, who finds his joy in himself and has no need to seek it outside of himself.

XIII. Angels and Demons

rom a natural point of view, demons operate like angels. Their fall did not cause loss of faculties or natural properties: they think and act as spirits. They can communicate their thought without the aid of sensible signs and can place matter into motion merely by their will. These modes of intellectual communication and spiritual operation are still proper to them as much as to the faithful angels.

Angels stay united to God, who is the illuminating principle of their intelligence and the directing principle of their operations, as the end where all of their activity flows. The others do not receive any illumination from him but have their activity from him as does any creature. However, they act against his divine plan, trying to disrupt it without success.

Angels are light; demons are darkness. The first group knows God's ways in the supernatural order: although God has reserved certain secrets that remain impenetrable to the angels themselves, he has largely initiated them into the great mysteries that concern the founding of his Kingdom on earth, i.e., the propagation of the Church, the salvation of souls. The angels, dwelling faithfully in the order of the divine plan, are its faithful stewards and executors.

Demons, due to their sin, are absolutely and irrevocably excluded from the order of grace. As a result, the mysteries of life and of supernatural actions are a completely sealed book to them. The realities of grace, being of divine order, are beyond any created spirit's comprehension; not even a good angel could penetrate it once reduced to its natural faculties. But in demons—rebellious, fallen spirits—there is not only powerlessness to comprehend the mysteries of the supernatural order but even opposition in grasping it. The essential disposition that prepares an intelligent creature to receive communication is humility, in other words, knowledge of one's nothingness. Yet the fallen spirit, the Devil, is a spirit of pride, in which there is a violent contradiction with anything that flows forth from divine grace. This diabolical wickedness places its fine intelligence in such a darkness as to render it clumsy and awkward.

Enlightened by God and dwelling in his justice, the good angels are superior to the evil ones. In the same way that the quality of being spiritual grants the possessor an undeniable superiority over the purely material being, so the quality of the just confers on the possessor a right of dominion over that which is unjust. St. Augustine affirms how "the deserting, sinful spirit" becomes necessarily dependent on the intelligence that remains upright and on the spirit that remains faithful. The angels have dominion over the demons, much more so than the great saints on earth do. This dominion consists in limiting the perversion of the spirits of darkness, repressing their bold attempts, and constraining them to keeping within the limits that God has set for them. Within those limits where the demons' bad influence is allowed to unfold, the angels redirect everything into the order of God's justice. We must never forget: not everything is permissible for the Devil, and where God does allow him to show his power, he ends up working—against his own intentions—for the final glorification of Jesus Christ and of his Church. The duty of the angels is to keep guard over the evil spirit lest he overstep his limited sphere of influence, as well as to affirm God's Providence in the crises that the Devil causes. We need only recall St. Michael, who hinders the Devil from revealing the location of Moses' tomb to the Hebrews lest they fall into idolatry, and St. Raphael, who ties up the impure demon Asmodeus!

These two scriptural facts establish the angels' supremacy over demons. The saints have dominion over both the Devil and his followers. Since they are humans, however, they are inferior to demons, demons being angelic spirits while the saints retain a fragile human nature, not immune from demonic influence, subject to their disruptions. The saints cannot say what Jesus could say of himself: "The ruler of the world is coming. He has no power over me" (Jn 14:30). This explains the Devil's power to torment them. At the same time, precisely because of their holiness, they are superior to him, gain control over him, and make him tremble.

Bound by the power of the good angels and controlled by the saints, the Devil then pounces on the sinner who hands himself over to him as food, just like St. Augustine writes: "*Datus est diabolo in cibum peccator*." In this case, demons have full dominion. Already superior to sinful men by nature, they possess them by right of conquest and by consent of abdication. Equal to angels by nature, conserving their purely spiritual mode of operation, demons yet remain irreversibly under the power of the blessed spirits by virtue of cosmic order or by Divine Providence, which decrees that the unjust, rebel spirit be subdued and governed by the just and faithful spirit.

XIV. Angelic Service

ngels are God's ministers and co-workers, and, as such, they are initiated into the divine mysteries. They read into the heavenly mind and know, at least generally, the reasons behind the direction of Providence. They see clearly why God allows evil and how he intends to manifest a greater good for the Church by permitting such-and-such a heresy, this schism, that apostasy. They work together to carry out the divine plan.

Independently of this general vision of the mysteries of the order of grace, they know particular realities related to the mission they are charged with accomplishing. The highest angels direct their inferiors, who know reality, whether as a whole or in part, through what is revealed to them by the higher ones.

Given these principles, it follows that angels can be ignorant of certain things, and that their knowledge, ample as it may be, cannot be compared to divine knowledge. They cannot penetrate the secret of souls. Barring an extraordinary revelation, they do not have absolute certainty whether this or that soul is in a state of grace, and much less whether or not a given human being numbers among the elect. The angels do not know, as Jesus has made clear, the hour of judgment; this is knowledge that depends on the number of the elect, because the hour of judgment will sound when God has gathered in the last of his chosen ones. This ignorance is dependent on the condition of being a creature and does not jeopardize the perfection of blessedness.

In order to fully embrace the action of angels, it is necessary to elevate one's thought to God, Father of the spirits, and to the Holy Spirit as well, inspirer of all good spirits. One must consider angels as part of the atmosphere surrounding the Holy Spirit in which he beams his primordial rays and makes them resound. These luminous waves, these melodious vibrations communicate with each other down to that limit of the spirit world where human intelligences hang drifting, half-bogged down in the darkness of matter. How these lights and these flames reach their higher or lower ranks in the celestial hierarchies is difficult to understand and even more so to explain. The Doctors of the Church tell us that the higher angels adapt themselves to the capacities of their inferiors, dividing the ray they themselves have received into a more substantial, comprehensive form.

In order to penetrate human intelligence, which takes its object from a sensible image, the divine ray has to be reflected and modified.

This is what Dionysius the Areopagite marvelously expresses when he teaches that, in us, the purest ray of truth is arrayed in a variety of sacred symbols.

We cannot handle the true light: it has to be tempered and colored in tones that help our all-too-weak eyes to rest. Now, the angels are the ones who transmit the divine ray, dressing it up in symbols and images in order to propose it to our intelligence.

The ray itself comes from God; the likenesses by which he tempers his glare come from the angels. The substance descends from the Father of Lights; its accidental, accommodating form is added by the heavenly spirits. Their role is similar to that of teachers, who simplify the truth according to their students' capacity by using comparisons and examples. Still, this angelic action is both interior and more efficacious. St. Bernard sees angels helping preachers of God's word: "In my opinion," he says, "they are not content with merely suggesting appropriate images interiorly, they also provide the clarity of language that makes the thought more easily and more pleasantly grasped; for preaching should be clear, noble, and even elegant in order to place and convince."

Angels, enlightening our intelligence, also touch our heart and give us holy inspirations. St. Bernard, commenting on the word of the Psalmist, "With their hands they shall support you" (Ps 91:12), shows us what angelic hands are. "By hands," he tells us, "we should understand a double-sided thought which they keep fixed in our heart, and which act as an immovable support to its left and to its right. On the one hand, this double thought is about the fleetingness of present things, and on the other, the lastingness of eternal things. The holy angels unceasingly whisper into our ear: "Despise all that passes, turn to what passes not!" They thus protect and quicken our race to heaven."

They also have a preventative duty toward our body. This is the literal sense of that passage St. Bernard was explaining allegorically, "With their hands they shall support you, lest you strike your foot against a stone."

XV. THE MALEVOLENT POWER OF DEMONS

The Devil, with his fall from heaven, lost grace but not his power and natural faculties. Still, his damned state, that is, his irrevocable separation from God, has limited the power and capacity of his intellective penetration.

The Devil does not understand the mysteries of grace, which are beyond any created intelligence and are in radical opposition to the arrogant, rebellious spirit.

While Jesus was on earth, the Devil could not grasp the innermost bond in him that united his human nature to the divine. He only saw the human Jesus and could not know with certainty that he was dealing with the coeternal Son of God. At times he made his conjectures through certain signs, and this is how the demons fled from the bodies of the possessed shouting: "What have you to do with us, Son of God?" (Mt 8:29). This expression does not yet imply an exact notion of the Second Divine Person. Often Jesus' normal, humble aspect confused and led this prideful spirit astray, and he no longer knew what to think. According to St. Paul, the Devil induced the Hebrews to crucify Jesus not knowing who he was:

"For if they had known it, they would not have crucified the Lord of glory" (1 Cor 2:8).

This is the same way that he deals with every saint and every one of the Lord's chosen ones, obviously in different proportions.

No more than he can comprehend the mystery of Jesus' divine sonship can he know the mystery of election and predestination that is hidden in God from before all ages and that is fulfilled in time. He does not know—he *cannot* know—who God's elect are. He is necessarily blocked by God's will, running up against inevitable defeat.

Moreover, he does not know who is in the state of grace and who isn't. He does not know up to what point sin has made its way, ignorant of what takes place in the penitent soul's conscience before God.

He recognizes them by how easily they follow him.

Let us then not exaggerate the idea that the Devil has such great power. The entire supernatural order is closed off to him by a dual mandate. Pride blinds this formidable power of his and makes it capable of all sorts of curses and iniquity.

What is there to worry about from the Devil, then? A penetration of the natural order, which it would be reckless not to be vigilant about.

Thanks to that subtlety that allows him to creep up to the very borders of the soul and body and to explore the influence and reactions exchanged between these two parts of our being, the Devil has profound knowledge of our capacities, our inclinations, our sympathies and antipathies, our dominant defect, our weak point—just the right way to sneak in a sentiment that will bring us down at a given moment.

He can just as easily inflame our imagination with the widest array of images and stir up our sensual passions. This power is greatly to be feared. It is necessary for God to keep him at bay and sustain us interiorly with his grace if we are going to be able to resist.

Pregnant with sin, like St. Paul says, the flesh is his ally; this world, where the triple concupiscence reigns, is his own dominion (1 Jn 5:19). His tempting reinforces the seductions of the flesh and the deceptions of the world.

He is present in every sin, in the sense that every sin is an imitation and, in a way, a development of the first sin he instigated. But it would be inaccurate to say that every sin is a result of his direct suggestions. All too often man is enough in and of himself to be distracted and seduced away from God.

The Devil retains his ability to act subtly over the creatures that make up the world, but God does not permit him to wield this power unless it is within the order of justice, and holds him to limits he cannot transgress.

In the Apocalypse there appear four angels who stand on the Euphrates and who, unbound by divine decree, wipe out a third of the human race. These are recognized as evil angels. If God were to allow the Devil to act as he wanted, with one zap he would empty earth of its inhabitants and knock it from its orbit!

The ancients saw the hand of evil angels behind scourges of all kinds.

Tertullian had a grandiose idea of the power of the Devil and his followers. Sicknesses, tragic accidents, delirium and madness, locust and plague, everywhere he saw a break in the balance of the world, he suspected the dark, corrupting work of demons. There is no doubt that these different incidents are not necessarily always brought about by demons, but they can be, and that suffices. Nothing happens without a reason, and nature alone does not explain everything.

XVI. The Nine Choirs of Angels

he separation of the evil angels from the good caused a void in what Scripture defines as the heavenly host. And as God could not leave a void in his most beautiful work, several theologians think that he created the human race in order to fill it, furnishing the heavenly Jerusalem with a determined number of the elect.

Whatever the case, and despite the treason by the rebel angels, the heavenly hosts still rank themselves according to their distinctions and the gifts allotted them from the beginning.

The angels do not all have the same degree of likeness to God; some participate more than others in the divine perfections. From their greater or lesser resemblance to the Creator, that is, from their more or less complete participation in his infinite perfections, we distinguish three hierarchies or spheres, subdivided into a total of nine distinct choirs of angels.

Sphere I	Sphere II	Sphere III
Choirs of *Serpahim*	Choirs of *Dominions*	Choirs of *Principalities*
Choirs of *Cherubim*	Choirs of *Virtues*	Choirs of *Archangels*
Choirs of *Thrones*	Choirs of *Powers*	Choirs of *Angels*

All these names are taken from Sacred Scripture, especially from St. Paul, while the distribution and reciprocal subordination of the angelic choirs are described by Dionysius the Areopagite, a Greek philosopher and theologian living between the end of the fourth and the beginning of the fifth century.

Regarding the angels of children, Jesus says, "Their angels in heaven always look upon the face of my heavenly Father" (Mt 18:10). Thus the humblest of the angels contemplate God face to face and are consequently united to him without intermediaries. The distinction between angels has nothing to do then with who does or does not have a direct and immediate relationship with God, but with which ones penetrate the Divine Essence before the others do and discover there the secrets that the inferior angels do not know except through their mediation. It is as if we were to imagine two people at the same show, one with sharper vision than the other: the latter can be informed by the former of those things that escape his weaker vision. This is the way that the inferior angels are enlightened by the superior angels on many mysterious things that they are incapable of knowing on their own, even though they enjoy the divine vision. The enlightenment that is passed from on high down through the ranks of the holy hierarchies does no harm to the intimate union of all the angels with God.

Division of the Angelic Choirs

The **first sphere** (or **hierarchy**) of angels receives everything from God without mediation; perfectly united to God to a very high degree, they uncover the divine secrets from those secrets' very source. Still, within such a strict, universal adhesion to the Most Holy Trinity, there are degrees that determine three distinct Choirs.

The first and highest, the one deepest in the furnace of the divine adorers, is that of the *seraphim*, whose name means *luminescent* and represents the perfection of Love.

The second, plunged in the ocean of Eternal Truth, is that of the *cherubim,* whose name means *fullness of knowledge* and represents the perfection of intelligence.

The third is called the choir of *thrones*, so called because God resides in them with all of his glory and with all of his majesty. They represent eternity and the immovable steadfastness of the Divine Being.

The unity of this marvelous hierarchy expresses the Divine Unity, and its diversity as three choirs adores the Trinity of Persons, since the Father seems to reside among the thrones, while the Word shines his splendor among the cherubim, and the Holy Spirit kindles the seraphim with a fire of eternal loves.

The **second sphere** sees God face to face. From the first sphere it receives communication about certain secrets that it is powerless to delve into on its own. The ardor of the seraphim helps these secondary angels to better love God; the knowledge of the cherubim initiates them into the depth of the mysteries; the steadfastness of the thrones serves to settle them in adoration of the divine perfections. This sphere seems dedicated to reflecting God's dominion to inferior beings. Hence the names of the three choirs that compose it: *dominions*, *virtues*, *powers*.

Dominions, with their imperturbable serenity, represent the incommunicable supremacy and the inalienable dominion of the Creator over all his works.

Virtues, with their penetrating activity, bring the secret, irresistible strength of divine operations to fruition.

Powers adore and also participate magnificently in the invincible power of God over the evil spirits, and thwart the efforts of the powers of darkness.

The **third sphere** is subordinated to the middle one. It is, more specifically than the second, the executor of the orders handed down from the superior angels. Just like the second sphere takes its passion, its light, and its elusive steadfastness from the first, this inferior hierarchy receives an investiture of authority from the second, a communication of strength, a flow of power. Exalted and strengthened this way, it easily manages the human race and the material world, without ever ceasing to enjoy the vision of God because of it. Its three choirs go by appreciable degrees.

Principalities are charged with the general guardianship of the peoples.

Archangels are employed for very important messages and events of high occasion.

Angels watch over individuals and enter the life of each person intimately.

The division of the hierarchies and choirs is not really the only harmoniously distinguishing element existing among the angels. They differ from one another, within one same heart, through characteristics proper to each one. With human beings, the difference is determined by the body, not by the soul. With angels, purely spiritual beings, it comes necessarily through certain spiritual properties that do not allow for confusion with one another. It is evident that the variety existing among their ranks is almost infinite.

Just as there are no two human faces that resemble each other exactly, there are no two angelic figures with identical features. The different choirs have a variety of colorations and luminescence, one from the other, that makes them like categories of precious stones that are in turn individually distinguished from each other by infinitely diverse, delicate hues.

According to the teaching of St. Thomas, the angels of the superior hierarchies are incomparably more numerous than those of the inferior ones. This is how he interprets the words of Sacred Scripture, "Thousands upon thousands were ministering to him, / and myriads upon myriads stood before him" (Dn 7:10). The angels who serve God, who carry out his orders, are those of the last choirs, while the angels who stand in his presence are those of the more elevated choirs. What Scripture seems to be implying is that the latter are *ten thousand times* more numerous than the former. What a revelation of the magnificence of heaven! The angelic choirs, as do the heavenly spheres, grow greater the closer they approach God.

XVII. St. Michael the Archangel

any exegetes consider St. Michael the head of the faithful angels, in opposition to Lucifer, head of the rebellious ones. Revelation tells us, "Then war broke out in heaven; Michael and his angels battled against the dragon" (Rev 12:7). This passage can indicate the daily, open battle between the good and evil angels, whose target is humanity's salvation or damnation; more specifically, the supreme struggle between the spirits of light and the spirits of darkness, which characterizes the world's end times but can easily be interpreted as the story of the first war over the Dragon's expulsion with his rebel angels, to whom heaven was closed forever.

This last interpretation seems even more compatible with the literal sense, since after this war "there was no longer any place for them in heaven." Besides, who cannot clearly see that, if Scripture points out a direct contention between St. Michael and Satan, this contention must go back to the origin of the universe?

St. Michael, then, is truly God's standard bearer in this great fight, "*Signifer Michael*." He is head of the heavenly armies that rallied in obedience to their Creator, "*Princeps militiae caelestis*." The faithful angels are called *his* angels, "*Michael et angeli ejus*." We can now see the greatness and beauty of this spirit of light, whose name expresses a victorious movement of adoration and love. In that magnificent moment all of the armies of heaven were drawn toward God.

St. Michael took over command of the faithful angels and played his part in all the plans of Providence for humanity. St. Gregory the Great could say, "Every time a marvelous event occurs, St. Michael's intervention appears."

St. Michael is also in charge of guardianship over the descendants of Abraham. Sacred Scripture teaches us that an angel spoke to Moses in the Lord's name, both in the burning bush and on the flaming height of Sinai, and that an angel was in charge of guarding the Hebrews' march toward the Promised Land. Who was this angel? He is not indicated by a special name, but at Moses' death it was St. Michael who appeared. St. Jude writes, "Yet the archangel Michael, when he argued with the devil in a dispute over the body of Moses, did not venture to pronounce a reviling judgment upon him but said, 'May the Lord rebuke you!'" (Jude 9). What does this mysterious passage mean? According to general opinion, the Devil wanted to make the resting place of the body of Moses, their great lawgiver, known to the Hebrews so that they would go and adore him. St. Michael, though, faithful executor of God's will, opposed this revelation and kept the great prophet's burial place a secret. St. Jude praises him for not having entertained a discussion and for having been content, in this case, with opposing the Devil's with God's authority.

St. Michael was the People of God's supreme guardian, and this is made more evident in a passage from Daniel. The prophet began a prolonged fast in order to learn from the Lord when the restoration of Jerusalem would take place. After three weeks of austere penance, he saw appear before him a figure of such terrifying majesty that he was unable to keep looking at him and fell face-down on the ground. It is an angel who lifts him up and consoles him, saying he is a messenger of the divine promises. He informs him that he has beseeched the Most High for the Hebrew prisoners' return. "But the prince of the kingdom of Persia stood in my way for twenty-one days, until finally Michael, one of the chief princes, came to help me." And he finishes by saying, "Soon I must fight the prince of Persia again. When I leave, the prince of Greece will come . . . No one supports me against these except Michael, your prince" (Dn 10:13; 20-21).

The meaning drawn from these passages is that everything happens within the Most High's counsel. There is a decision being made as to whether the Hebrews will reenter the Promised Land. One angel is requesting the prisoners' return but has as an adversary a figure described as "the prince of the kingdom of Persia." Is it a good or an evil spirit? He is thought to be a good spirit, placed in charge of guarding the Persian Empire and who, solicitous for the interests of those entrusted to him, tries to keep the Hebrews in a country where they will win adorers over to the true God. And so, of the two angels, one begs for the Hebrews' return to Judaea, the other for them to stay in Persia. The latter was supported by the angel of Greece and in general by those angels guarding the peoples where the Hebrew tribes had been dispersed. St. Michael intervenes and weighs the balance in favor of the Hebrews' return. He is their prince, and his voice has great weight in the Most High's counsels.

However, the prophet sees the distant future unfolding, and his vision reaches to those extreme trials reserved for God's People. "It shall be a time unsurpassed in distress," and yet, "at that time there shall arise Michael, / the great prince, / guardian of your people" (Dn 12:1).

St. Michael continues in the Church of Jesus Christ the protection that he assured the synagogue. He is in charge of defending it on the course of its pilgrimage here below and will make it triumph in the supreme battle that awaits at the end of days.

According to wise interpreters, St. Michael the Archangel is the spirit who, according to St. Paul, will issue forth as if from the lips of the Lord Jesus and slay the Antichrist (2 Thes 2:8).

The Church is not ungrateful to its heavenly protector: it makes glorious reference to him in the liturgy and gives him the most beautiful descriptors the

Apocalypse offers, placing in his hands the golden censer that sends the prayers of the holy ones to God. It hears him sound the trumpet while St. John contemplates the sacred mystery; it feels him in the earthquake and churning sea when he descends from heaven; it points to the hanging, celestial standards and the hushed angelic choirs when he fights against the Devil; it calls upon him to aid all the sons of God, invokes him under the title Spirit of Wisdom and Intelligence, makes him prince of the angelic hosts—*Praepositus Paradisi*, the provost, that is, the priest of paradise, whom the inhabitants of the Heavenly Jerusalem glorify, whose honor lies in bestowing gifts on all the nations, and whose prayer rises high to the Kingdom of Heaven. As prince, he is escorted by a multitude of angels. God entrusts the souls of his holy ones to him so that he will lead them into the eternal joy of paradise. This great standard-bearer of God, having snatched them from the jaws of the infernal lion, brings them into the holy light that will enthrall them for eternity.

The word of Daniel can be translated into Latin as "*Unus de Principibus primis.*" According to many interpreters, this is a Hebraicism equivalent to: "*Primus inter primos.*" St. Michael would then be the first among the first angels, or, more simply, the first of all angels. The title of *archangel* given to St. Michael is a general term for his preeminence, and, far from simply meaning that he belongs to the second angelic choir, it points out that he is the first of the seraphim, the one most united to God.

The intervention of the glorious archangel seems necessary whenever dangers loom greatest. Pope Leo XIII composed a beautiful invocation: "St. Michael the Archangel, defend us in battle, be our protection against the wickedness and snares of the Devil. May God rebuke him, we humbly pray. And do thou, O Prince of the Heavenly Host, by the Power of God, thrust into hell Satan and all evil spirits who wander the earth seeking the ruin of souls." Such an invocation was also recommended by Pope John Paul II. More than ever an unbridled Satan is raising his head; to subdue him and force him back into the abyss, we need the arm of St. Michael. The success of the battle has been indicated from the beginning. The archangel's glorious victory is eternal.

Titles of the Archangel Michael

✢ Protector of the Church
✢ Great Prince
✢ Prince of the Angelic Hosts
✢ Prince of the Hebrew People
✢ Prince and Protector of the Christian People
✢ First Among the Great Princes

XVIII. St. Gabriel the Archangel

At the name St. Gabriel, the mind turns instantly to those paintings of the mystery of the Annunciation where he is depicted, lilies in hand, entering the confines of the house where Mary prays in silence. His name evokes the indescribable scene that would lead to the Incarnation of the Word.

Gabriel is the messenger par excellence of the Good News. His mission is to announce a Gospel (Lk 1:19).

During Old Testament times he began the preaching of this angelic Gospel as a preface to the human Gospel.

At the end of the captivity, God raised up in Babylon Daniel, one of the four great prophets. He is on fire for love of his people and brings the sin of his brethren before God. His heart is open wide and consumed by such strong desire for his people's liberation that he merits the touching name of "man of desires." St. Gabriel is sent to Daniel to relieve somewhat the thirst of desire that causes his prayers, his fasting, and his tears. In a vision, he reveals to Daniel the destinies of God's Kingdom on earth. He shows him the approaching arrival of the Holy of holies, who will put an end to iniquity and fulfill the prophecies. He reveals the precise date of this apparition of the Messiah: it will take place in "seventy weeks of years." This clear prophecy is the cornerstone of the Hebrews, convincing them irrefutably of the Savior's coming and, at the same time, announcing their inevitable diaspora (Dn 9).

However, the times are coming, the mysterious cycle of weeks spoken of in Daniel are almost fulfilled. After a long interval during which all communication seems suspended between heaven and earth, Gabriel is again on the scene: he goes to the Temple in Jerusalem, at the hour when the priest burned incense before the Most High, perhaps at the same hour of the evening sacrifice when he had approached Daniel. The priest in service at the temple was a just, God-fearing man named Zechariah. He notices the archangel standing to the right of the altar of incense. He is terrorized, but Gabriel reassures him and foretells the joyful news that he, despite his age, will be the father of a child destined to be the forerunner of the Messiah. Zechariah hesitates in his belief and is struck mute. His tongue will be loosened only once his son is born (Lk 1:9-20).

Six months later, the Archangel Gabriel again sets out. This time he heads for Galilee, visiting a young woman of the royal stock of David, who lives in poverty and has remained a virgin under the veil of a chaste marriage. He introduces himself to her with infinite respect as an ambassador of the Most Holy Trinity. The salvation of the world is entrusted by him into the hands of a Virgin; if she gives her consent, heaven will be opened and the Savior will descend. Mary, in her humility, is perplexed, but the angel reassures her.

She hesitates, and the archangel calms her worry. The celestial ambassador is successful; he obtains her consent. With an act of heroic faith, she draws within herself the Son of God and gives him flesh.

According to a beautiful expression from the ancients, Gabriel is truly the *Paranymph* of the wedding between the Word and humanity. This was the title of the friend in charge of leading the groom into the marriage chamber. St. Gabriel led the Heavenly Groom into the marriage chamber that was the womb of the Virgin Mary, where the Word was wedded to our nature.

Is it enough to consider him the Messenger of the Good News, as the evangelist from heaven to earth? His beautiful name, "the Strength of God," reveals an even more profound duty.

Man on his own shrinks back in the presence of the supernatural; it frightens and disturbs him. He trembles in contact with God, is too weak to support the divine light. Who will step in to reassure, strengthen, and *acclimate* him to the communication

God wants to have with him? In general, this is left to the good angels, in particular Gabriel, whose name expresses a transmission of divine strength. In fact, if we open the Holy Scriptures, we see him sent to strengthen the souls of his chosen ones and saints.

He supports Daniel, who initially falls face-first to the ground at Gabriel's truly gleaming appearance (Dn 8:15). If, as many scholars think, Gabriel should be recognized as the one who works out the return from captivity, it is he who again reassures the prophet, filling him with divine force. "Do not fear, beloved [*lit.* 'man of desires']," he says. "Peace! Take courage and be strong." And the prophet answers, "Speak, my lord, for you have strengthened me" (Dn 10:19).

Do not fear. It is the Archangel Gabriel's favorite phrase. He repeats it to Zechariah and to the Blessed Virgin. These are no empty words in his mouth; it has powerful efficacy.

At the sight of the archangel, Zechariah is not only disturbed but terrified. The angel tries to calm him—"Do not fear"—then reveals the divine oracle concerning him. Zechariah hesitates to believe, and he is not free from blame: the angel's word was meant to produce perfect faith in him.

The Vigin Mary's attitude was a very different story. She is better able to withstand the sight of the archangel than was Zechariah; the supernatural does not surprise or intimidate her. She remains unfrightened, she is merely perturbed by the unusual nature of his greeting: "*Ne timeas, Maria*." We have to wonder at the effect of these words. Many Fathers tell us that they strengthened the Virgin's soul, at the same time that they caused her to make a heroic act of faith and trust and to support the unfathomable mystery that was ready to come about in her.

"Gabriel is called the Strength of God," St. Bernard tell us, "both because he announced the descent of Divine Virtue in the presence of the Savior, and because he had the mission of comforting the Virgin, shy and modest by nature, in such a way that the novelty of the mystery would not frighten her. That is precisely what he did."

Under Mary's shy exterior lay a strong, fearless soul. It is ordained by Providence that the human creature should receive help from the angelic creature. Therefore, with his message from the Most Holy Trinity, the archangel had the mission of communicating to Mary an increase in supernatural vitality to meet her sublime role as Mother of the Word.

We read in the Gospel how "to strengthen him an angel from heaven appeared" to our Savior in the moment when his humanity was weakened and agonizing under the unbearable weight of our sins and of divine wrath (Lk 22:43). If Jesus accepted being comforted by an angel in his humanity, Mary most certainly could have been so in the reaction of her humility and virginal modesty. It was the same angel that both encouraged Jesus and comforted Mary: Gabriel.

The archangel, "Strength of God," is invoked by the Church to spurn the ancient enemy. Due to his appearance to Daniel "at the time of the evening sacrifice" and to Zechariah "standing to the right of the altar of incense," it considers him the angel of prayer and invites him to visit our churches to prepare the hearts of believers for divine communications. Perhaps St. Gabriel is the angel that presides at the Eucharistic sacrifice and is responsible for presenting the holy gifts to God's "altar in heaven."

XIX. St. Raphael the Archangel

he story of the Archangel Raphael is recounted in the Book of Tobit. The prologue presents the aged Tobit as an upright, eminently patient man, even through his multiple sufferings.

Wracked with sorrow, this old Israelite's soul is lifted to God in humble, fervent prayer. At that very moment, a young woman named Sarah, also a descendant of Abraham and daughter of Raguel, prays to the Lord through her tears: she begs to be set free from a deeply unsettling trial. Both the prayer of the old man and that of the young woman are recited at the same time by the angels in front of God's throne, who deigns to answer them. "So Raphael was sent to heal them both" (Tb 3:17).

Raphael's name means *Healer of God*. He takes on the appearance of a young Israelite man, Azariah, son of the great Hananiah, and greets Tobit's son Tobiah, who is looking for a guide for a long journey. The two set out with the blessings and well-wishes of the old man.

An accident happens. Tobiah, arriving at the bank of the Tigris River, wishes to refresh his tired feet in the water. Without warning an enormous fish rushes at him. He cries for help. "Grab the fish and hold on to it!" says the angel. The young man obeys and drags the fish from the water. "Slit the fish open and take out its gall, heart, and liver, and keep them with you; but throw away the other entrails. Its gall, heart, and liver are useful for medicine," the angel then says. Setting back out on the journey, Tobiah questions his companion. "Brother Azariah, what medicine is in the fish's heart, liver, and gall?" He answers, "As for the fish's heart and liver, if you burn them to make smoke in the presence of a man or a woman who is afflicted by a demon or evil spirit, any affliction will flee and never return. As for the gall, if you apply it to the eyes of one who has white scales, blowing right into them, sight will be restored" (Tb 6).

The two travelers arrive at Rages where the young Sarah, daughter of Raguel, lives. She is beset by a demon that, on each of her seven wedding nights, has killed the husbands that her parents have chosen for her. At the angel's advice, Tobiah courageously asks for her hand in marriage and is accepted. Thanks to his chaste intention and the smoke rising from the heart and liver of the fish as it burns on the coals, he is not killed like the others. This smoke chases away the demon, who only has power over the lustful. St. Raphael then captures him and ties him up helpless in the desert of Upper Egypt.

This is the first healing the angel performs. The second concerns Tobit, blind for a long time now, who anxiously awaits the return of his beloved son.

At the angel's prompting, Tobiah sprinkles the fish's gall on his father's eyes, and hc recovers his sight.

How could this family not be grateful toward this miraculous healer! His mission is accomplished, and he finally reveals himself. "I am Raphael, one of the seven angels who stand and serve before the Glory of the Lord." Everyone is shaken at these words, and they all fall face to the ground. "Do not fear; peace be with you!," the angel says. "'Bless God now and forever. As for me, when I was with you, I was not acting out of any favor on my part, but by God's will. So bless God every day; give praise with song. Even though you saw me eat and drink, I did not eat or drink anything; what you were seeing was a vision. So now bless the Lord on earth and give thanks to God. Look, I am ascending to the one who sent me. Write down all that has happened to you.' And he ascended" (Tb 12).

This farewell so surprised those present that they remained for hours with their faces to the ground, blessing and praising God.

The Archangel Raphael was sent with a twofold aim: to heal the eyes of the old Tobit and to free the young Sarah from the infestation of a demon. He is obliged to fulfill his mission. He appears in human form, concealing his ethereal nature, just as he hides his healing action under the guise of natural remedies. One fish provides the elements of a double, miraculous cure: the burned heart and liver drive out the demon Asmodeus, while the gall heals the eyes of Tobit, afflicted with cataracts.

The ancients believed that the gall of a certain fish called *collonymus* had the power to heal eyes; this is, in fact, the opinion reported by Dioscorus, Galen, and Pliny. We can easily suppose that the angel was trying to cover up his supernatural action under a natural property. The way in which the cure took place is evidently through an effective application of fish gall, but we must agree that the angel added some sort of special property. Blindness cannot be cured so easily with a mere, natural remedy.

It is harder to grasp the suppositions surrounding the smoke of the heart and liver burning on the coals, and the expulsion of the impure demon. Should we then deny the link between them? The demon's action is bound to certain objects that he has put under his influence but is chased out by the use of blessed objects of a determined nature. It is not without reason that certain substances are mixed with water to be used for exorcisms and blessings. The material used evidently has some secret link with the effect they are called to produce, even if they do not have supernatural effects in and of themselves. This is how the smoke of the burning heart and liver worked to diffuse the demon's attempt. By its pungency it quenches the lust that normally feeds off of the sweet smell of perfumes. Moreover, the archangel was there to activate its desired effect, and he was then able to use his strength to capture the demon Asmodeus: he tied him up and abandoned him in the desert of Upper Egypt.

Raphael tied up the demon of impurity, the spirit of fornication from which the Church asks the Lord to free her children: Asmodeus, whose name means either "fire of Media" or "fire of devastation," since the vice of impurity putrefies the soul and leaves destruction like a fiery wind. This demon held power over all the men who had entered the marriage with unchaste intentions: he physically suffocated them.

Challenging this demon stood Raphael, who thus appears as the angel of purity, of virginal hearts, and of chaste unions. Calming the passions of the soul, he shows himself as the true *Healer of God*.

On this archangel's former feast day of October 24 (now joined with Gabriel and Michael on September 29), the Church used to read the episode of the pool of Bethesda reported by the Gospel of John (Jn 5:1-9) to make us understand that the celestial healer Raphael had not limited his kindnesses to the family of Tobit but had continued to shower them on Israel.

Around the time of Passover, the "*Angel of the Lord*" used to descend into this pool, and his entrance was marked by an unusual movement of the water. The first ill person to emerge was the one healed. The Church holds that this healing angel was Raphael.

How not to believe that this archangel does not perform his duty of mercy on the Church itself? Even if he does so perhaps more secretly, there is little doubt that he does so more effectively than under the Old Law. Tobit's family is a symbol of the Church, within which Raphael spiritually continues the effects of his powerful intervention. He puts an end to the evildoing of the impure demon, stops him from harming the true children of Abraham, supports the holiness of marriage, protects the integrity of virgins, and puts them in union with Jesus. He heals the eyes of the blind, enlightens souls with prophetic clarity, and inspires believers to praise God and to bless him for his merciful works. To sum up, he guards us on our earthly pilgrimage and leads us to those horizons where we can begin to see the brilliantly shining Jerusalem (Tb 13:16-18).

The names of the archangels have precise meaning in their etymologies:

✣ **Michael**: "Who is like God?"
✣ **Gabriel**: "Strength of God"
✣ **Raphael**: "Medicine of God"

XX. The Seven Angels Before the Throne of God

S t. John, at the beginning of Revelation, makes the following greeting: "John, to the seven churches in Asia: grace to you and peace from him who is and who was and who is to come, and from the seven spirits before his throne" (Rev 1:4).

This passage teaches us that, in the midst of all these myriads of millions of angels in God's presence, as the prophet Daniel tells us, there are seven who stand at his Throne like great court officials, as seven burning lampstands that burn before the majesty of the Most High without being consumed.

The prophet Zechariah had caught sight of them in the vision of the mysterious stone on which seven eyes appeared: "On this one stone with seven facets ["eyes"] I will engrave its inscription—oracle of the LORD of hosts—and I will take away the guilt of that land in one day" (Zec 3:9).

St. John stares at these eyes curiously after there appears to him "a Lamb that seemed to have been slain. He had seven horns and seven eyes; these are the [seven] spirits of God sent out into the whole world" (Rev 5:6).

The agreement between the prophet and the apostle is perfect. There are seven blessed spirits connected with the sacred humanity of the Savior, as if identifying with it. These are represented by symbols of seven horns—emblem of strength and power—or by seven eyes—emblem of untiring vigilance that extends throughout the earth.

We do not know all the names of these angelic spirits.

St. Gabriel makes it known to Zechariah that he is one of the seven: "I am Gabriel, who stand before God" (Lk 1:19). St. Raphael declares it formally speaking to Tobit's family: "I am Raphael, one of the seven angels who stand and serve before the Glory of the Lord" (Tb 12:15).

This affirmation on the part of Raphael is decisive for interpreting the Book of Revelation. Certain authors have written that the seven spirits stood for the seven gifts in which the Holy Spirit seems to multiply himself, or even the assisting angels grouped together in general under the symbolic number of seven. In reality, there do exist seven individual angels more closely bonded than any others to the Savior's sacred humanity.

Different authors also place St. Michael in this honorable cohort along with SS. Gabriel and Raphael; the names of the others remain a mystery.

Jesus is surrounded by this angelic cohort. When God sent his Word to earth, he commanded his angels to adore him, says St. Paul (Heb 1:6), making him an escort by collecting seven guardians around his body, chosen from among the highest officials of the celestial court. This is how *God's Only Begotten* appeared in this world. The seven angels appear again in various passages of the Apocalypse: they sound the seven trumpets; they pour the seven cups of divine vengeance out upon the earth. St. John sees them leaving the temple "dressed in clean white linen, with a gold sash around their chests" (Rev 15:6).

It cannot be certain that these executors of divine vengeance are the same that stand at God's throne. Raphael and Gabriel seem destined for a terrible role. It is possible that the angels of the seven trumpets and the seven cups are subordinates of the seven blessed spirits that act as the eyes of the Savior's sacred humanity.

Let us admire, at this point, how the earthly hierarchy imitates the celestial hierarchy. Above, there are seven angels, seven seals, seven trumpets, and seven cups; here below, there are seven churches and their seven bishops, even called angels, symbolized by the golden candelabras among which the Lord moves, and the seven stars that he holds in his hand.

Are the seven angels honored in the Church that they protect? Publicly there is no specific, common devotion to them other than that given to the angels in general; there are, however, traces of a local and especially private devotion.

In Palermo there once was a very ancient church dedicated to the seven angels who stood at God's Throne. There was also once a pious Sicilian priest, Don Antonio Lo Duca, who went to Rome with the purpose of spreading devotion to the seven angels. It was the year 1527. It was there, after much prayer and fasting, that he learned by a divine revelation that the Baths of Diocletian were to host the cult of the seven blessed spirits. The pope at that time shared the priest's passion. And so, in 1551, the imposing ruins of the baths were first consecrated in honor of St. Mary of the Angels or, rather, of the Blessed Virgin escorted by the seven angels. Very soon the work to complete and beautify the church was undertaken by none other than Michelangelo Buonarroti. The dedication was done by Pope Pius IV, who entrusted custody of the monument to the Carthusians.

Numerous possessed people were freed by the intercession of the seven angels, who escort the Blessed Virgin just as they do Jesus. The guards of the King's body are also officials to the Queen.

Let us honor them, and we will be following the liturgical spirit of the Church. Both St. Irenaeus and St. Cyprian mention them with respect, and Clement of Alexandria calls them "the First-born Princes of the

Angelic Hosts." Cardinal Bona addresses this prayer to them: "Spirits of holiness, you seven that stand in the presence of God, purify me, enlighten me, perfect me. Be my consolation in death, just as you are my defense in life. Diffuse within my spirit a godly light that, after absorbing all in me that is darkness, will burn with a love all divine."

According to the teaching of St. Anthony, there are seven main demons in charge of the seven deadly sins. The seven angels must be their luminous antagonists. And just as Raphael bound the impure demon Asmodeus with his strong arm, each one of them must be successfully battling against one of the heads of the army of evil.

XXI. ATTENDANT ANGELS AND MINISTERING ANGELS

he Holy Angels are divided into two categories: attendant and ministering. This distinction is taken from a vision of Daniel. "As
I watched, / Thrones were set up / and the Ancient
of Days took his throne. / His clothing was white
as snow, / the hair on his head like pure wool; / his
throne was flames of fire, / with wheels of burning
fire. / A river of fire surged forth, / flowing from where
he sat; thousands upon thousands were ministering
to him, / and myriads upon myriads stood before
him" (Dn 7:9-10). So there are a considerable number
of angels whose duty is to serve God, to carry out
his will; these are the ministering angels. In multiple
times greater number are those whose only duty consists in adoring and praising his infinite majesty. But
what is the nature of this distinction? Is it simply a
question of fact, in the sense that, from among all the
angels there are some sent on mission while the vast
majority remain in heaven before the presence of the
thrice-holy God? Or is it a distinction of office, in the
sense that some are employed for external ministry
while the others form a sort of court of honor around

the adorable Trinity, in the same way that there are active orders and contemplative orders on earth?

Dionysius the Areopagite and St. Thomas Aquinas affirm the distinction of office. According to these great Church theologians, not all the angels are sent on mission, only the ones from the last hierarchy; these, properly said, are the ministering angels. The angels of the two superior hierarchies remain invariably dedicated to the Person of God, their only function being to adore.

Can it at least be said that the angels of the superior hierarchies are sent on mission only in exceptional cases? No, responds St. Thomas. The coordination of the angelic choirs, being regulated by both grace and nature at the same time, does not allow for exceptions. Here below, the intervention of race can suspend the action of natural laws for an instant; but above, the orders of grace and nature are commingled and, consequently, the first never ends up altering the second.

The gifts of God therefore descend invariably by hierarchical means: from higher angels to lower angels, from lower angels to mankind. Consequently, human beings are never in a direct relationship with higher angels. Such is St. Thomas's reasoning. Still, one must recognize that there are strong theological objections worth raising against his theory.

1) St. Paul, speaking of the angels, says, "Are they not all ministering spirits sent to serve, for the sake of those who are to inherit salvation?" (Heb 1:14).
2) Holy Scripture declares that the Archangel Raphael, although coming here below to heal Tobit, is one of the seven spirits who stand before God.
3) For centuries the Church has offered this prayer to the angels: "Oh God, you who have at your command the ministering of angels and of men, grant us that our life may be defended by those same angels who perpetually await your bidding in Heaven."
4) Finally, it seems that if the Son of God has come down to earth personally for the salvation of mankind, then even the higher angels can be employed for humanity's redemption.

It would be too much to discuss these objections here one by one. Dionysius and St. Thomas have not left them without reply. They do recognize that the higher angels have interest in and are in some way employed in the salvation of souls and in directing human affairs, yet they are firm in stating that they do not act directly and immediately on earth. We feel their action only through the intermediation of lower angels, who represent them more or less explicitly, and they carry out certain works with their power and in their name.

What is certain is that the angels are indeed in relationship with us, that we are in contact with them.

XXII. Some Pious Devotions to Angels

chille Maria Triacca, a Salesian of holy memory, wrote in the entry on *angels* in the *Pauline Liturgical Dictionary* (2001) that "if one were to trace the history of the liturgical year's development, one would come upon a period when some local liturgies of the Roman tradition contemplated the cycle of the angels." He is speaking of Sundays called "before" or "after" the Sunday of the Angels. This feast day usually fell around the end of September or the beginning of October. This was the origin of the current practice of popular piety that dedicates the month of October to the angels. For centuries there have been angelic devotional texts for that month, texts that disappeared in the 1950s and of which no new ones have been composed.

Not only is there a month dedicated to the heavenly spirits but also a specific day of the week; since the fifteenth century it has been Monday. Some celebrate it on Tuesday (the founder of *Opus Dei*, **St. Josémaria Escrivá de Balaguer**, for example).

However, Monday became "Angel Day," gradually, when the day after the day consecrated to the Most Holy Trinity was reserved for the Heavenly Spirits.

In ancient times, the guardian angels were honored together with St. Michael, Captain of the Heavenly Armies: September 29 in the West, May 8 in the East. Gradually over time, a special feast was established just in their honor.

In 1513 it was introduced into the Kingdom of Portugal, yet it had already been celebrated in Spain, albeit at varying days and months. March 1 was the date accepted by the most important Churches and by the military and regular Orders.

Blessed François d'Estaing, bishop of Rodez, France (1460-1529), following the Spanish custom, adopted March 1 as the celebration of the guardian angel in his diocese and commissioned the Franciscan Jean Colombi to redact a special office in honor of the holy angels. The holy bishop also managed to obtain a papal bull from Pope Leo X, dated April 18, 1518, gaining approval for the feast that he had added to his diocesan calendar.

At the request of Ferdinand II of Austria, Pope Paul V, on September 27, 1608, instituted a solemn feast and an office proper for the guardian angels. The pontiff made the feast obligatory for all the States of the Austrian Empire, but he let it remain optional for other nations.

The feast's date was fixed for the first free day after the feast of St. Michael, which is September 29. Leo XIII, on July 5, 1883, elevated the feast to "double major" class, and a Decree on August 27, 1893, made it a primary feast.

The Archangel Gabriel used to be celebrated on March 24; Raphael, October 24; and St. Michael, September 29. With the liturgical reforms authorized by Vatican II, in an effort to eliminate redundancies in favor of a *sobria semplicitas*, we now have one feast, **September 29**, dedicated to all three of the Archangels Michael, Gabriel, and Raphael, and **October 2** dedicated to the recognition of the guardian angels.

Finally, of note is the fact that **Pope Sixtus V**, on February 5, 1590, granted an office in honor of the guardian angel to the Kingdom of Portugal and to all of its colonies; even today, with the permission of **Pope Pius XII**, Portuguese-speaking countries celebrate this feast on June 10.

As regards the *particular prayers for angels*, the ***Angelic Chaplet*** is widespread in Latin countries. It is composed of nine groups of three beads each; on each of these beads a Hail Mary is recited in honor of the Queen of Angels and of one specific angelic choir, with the intercession of St. Michael, and a prayer is made for a specific virtue inherent to each choir. The three beads of the Hail Mary are separated by one on which the Our Father is prayed in honor of the angel's Creator.

According to the tradition, the Angelic Chaplet hails from Portugal, where the Archangel St. Michael revealed it in person to his devotee **Blessed Antonia d'Astonac**, by all accounts a cloistered Carmelite nun. He promised her that whoever recited the chaplet before Communion would have, at the moment of receiving the Host, one angel from each of the angel choirs at their side. Furthermore, the Prince of the Heavenly Armies promised to whomever daily recites the Angelic Chaplet the assistance of the holy angels in life and, after death, the liberation of his or her soul and those of relatives from the pains of Purgatory. The Angelic Chaplet had a good following in Italy in the 1800s, thanks both to the Carmelite monastery of Vetralla and to the Theatine Fathers of St. Gaetano of Thiene (1480-1547) of the Basilica of St. Paul in Naples.

As regards litanies, after the Most Holy Trinity, the Blessed Virgin as Queen of Angels, and St. Joseph come the invocations of the three archangels and of all the holy orders of heavenly spirits.

Finally, there is the *Via Angelica*, a pious devotion composed and illustrated by Maestro Rolando Quaranta. Its form is based on the *Via Crucis*, following Sacred Scripture's accounts of angelic apparitions.

CONCLUSION

very evening, before going to bed with the Office of Compline, the Church asks the faithful to pray for God to send his angels to guard us in peace.

The angels have a very important duty, that of establishing peace in the world and in the Church, as well as in every soul born to this earth.

Peace, first and foremost, is the repose of the soul in truth and charity. The angels are the true enlighteners of our intelligence, and they strive to help us know God and his ways. Untiring in their work of light, they take advantage of the smallest circumstances of daily life: a moment of grief, a homily, a reading, a film . . . They help us understand the words we read and the events we witness. If we grow weak, they support us; if we tremble, they reassure us; if we sin, they pick us up and set us back on the right path; they never fail to encourage us toward good; they help our enthusiasm with our duties and spur us on to holiness. Only Christians who live familiarly with their angels can truly appreciate the power, goodness, and delicate generosity of these blessed, heavenly spirits.

Corresponding in like measure to their zeal for our eternal salvation, should be our devotion to them.

In order to inspire the faithful to an ever more ardent devotion, the Church has instituted feasts in their honor (September 29; October 2; May 8); has introduced them into the litanies and into the celebration of the Holy Mass; cites them in the *Catechism*; and has approved some prayers such as the Angel of God and the Angelic Chaplet.

Throughout the centuries the Church has seen poets rise to sing of them, and artists, painters, and sculptors depict these "envoys" of God. In this way devotion to angels, especially guardian angels, has become one of the most characteristic devotions of Catholicism with respect to other Christian traditions and other religions. To lose such a devotion or let it diminish means losing one of the most notable, beautiful aspects of the Catholic religion and also means that others, in our place, will speak or write of the angels—but they will no longer be those of the Bible, of the Most Holy Trinity, of the Father, of the Son, and of the Holy Spirit, nor of the mystics: they will be the angels of magic and of the occult.

Bibliography

Battista, M. *In cammino con gli angeli.* Bologna: Edizioni Dehoniane, 1994.

Bonaventura da Sorrento, *Michael.* Foggia: Edizioni Michael, 1994.

Bussagli, M. *Angeli: Origini, storie e immagini delle creature celesti.* Milan: Electa Mondadori, 2006.

Catechism of the Catholic Church. Vatican City: Libreria Editrice Vaticana, 1992.

Daniélou, J. *Gli angeli e la loro missione.* Milan: Gribaudi Editore, 1998.

Dionysius the Areopagite, *Tutte le opere.* Milan: Edizioni Rusconi, 1997.

Dizionario di mistica, s.v. angeli. Edited by L. Borriello, E. Caruana, M.R. Del Genio, N. Suffi. Vatican City: Libreria Editrice Vaticana, 1998.

Eiximenis, F. *Il Libro degli angeli.* Milan: Gribaudi Editore, 1999.

Faure, Ph. *Gli angeli.* Milan: San Paolo Edizioni, 1991.

Gozzelino, G. *Inchiesta sugli angeli.* Elledici, Turin 1987.

Guardini, R. *L'angelo*. Brescia: Morcelliana, 1994.

Hebert, A.J. *L'Arcangelo san Michele: Vita e apparizioni fino ai giorni nostri*. Udine: Edizioni Segno, 2009.

Jovanovic, P. *Il grande libro degli angeli custodi*. Casale Monferrato: Piemme, 2003.

Marconcini, B., A. Amato, C. Roccetta, M. Fiori, *Angeli e Demoni. Il dramma della storia tra il bene e il male*. Bologna: Ed. Dehoniane, 1992.

McKenna, M. *Angeli*. Milan: San Paolo Edizioni, 1997.

Peterson, E.—Manzi, F. *Il libro degli angeli: Gli esseri angelici nella Bibbia, nel culto e nella vita cristiana*. Rome: Centro Liturgico Vincenziano, 2008

Pope John Paul II, *Gli angeli*. Foggia: Edizioni Michael, 1986.

Sbaffoni, F. *San Tommaso d'Aquino e l'influsso degli angeli*. Bologna: Edizioni Studio Domenicano, 1993.

Shellier, H. *Principati e Potestà*. Brescia: Morcelliana, 1970.

Stanzione, M. *Trecentosessantacinque giorni con i tre Arcangeli Michele, Gabriele e Raffaele*. Udine: Edizioni Segno, 2009.

___. *Il ritorno degli angeli oggi: Tra devozione e mistificazione*. Udine: Edizioni Segno, 2007.

___. *La Via angelica. Itinerario verso Dio in compagni dei Santi angeli*. Milan: Edizioni Gribauldi, 2004.

Thorel, G. *Angeli*. Udine: Edizioni Segno, 1997.

Tuniz, D. *San Michele al Gargano*. Milan: Edizioni San Paolo, 1997.

Westermann, C. *Gli angeli di Dio non hanno bisogno di ali*. Casale Monferrato: Piemme, 1995.

Zanoletti, G. *Angeli: Messaggeri di Dio*. Milan: Piero Gribaudi Editore, 2003.